Centralized Blockchain for e-Governance: Revolutionizing Public Services with KryptOm

AUTHORS:-

DR(ER) OM PRAKASH

Professor, SMS Lucknow

ABSTRACT

This article suggests that the state of the art in the Civil Law traditions is not yet ready to produce a coherent and transversal answer to address the regulation of crypto-currencies. In general, legislators and lawmakers should aim to produce the rules necessary to achieve meticulously defined and explicit policy goals with respect to the virtual goods. In the article possible shortcomings of using the existing legal concepts to regulate crypto-currencies are highlighted. Additionally, it is shown that in practice, and financially, they have not yet achieved the necessary enhancement to force traditional concepts used to regulate fiat currency on crypto-currencies. The argument goes in line with previous literature that claims that current suggestions to regulate crypto-currencies do not risk inhibiting their development.

Keywords: Crypto-currencies; Bitcoin; economic regulation; Civil Law

INTRODUCTION

The traditional laws are not yet ready to generate a coherent and transversal response to regulate crypto-currencies and, in general, virtual goods. The restrictive regulatory responses that seek to avoid their misuse should be punctual and minimum necessary to comply with strictly defined policy objectives. Many countries, including India, have not yet developed the appropriate conceptual categories to regulate such a new phenomenon. Furthermore, from a practical and financial point of view, crypto-currencies have not reached sufficient importance to justify the regulatory effort that traditional currencies demand. This argument joins other voices that have warned with suggestions to regulate crypto-currencies, rather than inhibiting their development (Kaplanov, 2012). The concern that motivates this article is that in order to regulate Bitcoin, for example, the most popular crypto-currency, one ends up clumsily regulating the local Bitcoin exchanges or new applications of Blockchain, which is the technology that enables Bitcoin. Although in this article the attempt is not to address the problem of disruption and competition that has been the focus in countries like Chile, like the battle between crypto-currency intermediaries and traditional commercial banking, the attempt is rather to illustrate why crypto-currencies are a challenge for traditional law that it goes far beyond its potential criminal uses or the difficulties it presents for monetary regulation.

The development of the argument is based on the review of the concept of virtual currencies to distinguish them from other forms of electronic money. Crypto-currencies are revolutionary and therefore it is necessary to distinguish them from it. Crypto-currencies and virtual currencies not only share the characteristic of being digital, but both were designed to emulate the scarcity that exists in the real world. This is essential to understand the phenomenon to be regulated. In this regard, the operation of crypto-currencies are also illustrated to bring forth the aspects in which they represent something totally new for which many of our legal institutions are not adapted. If the law serves to attribute responsibilities or give certainty to the parties in a transaction, crypto-currencies have programmed in a way that could render many of the legal institutions that seek compliance or regulate the behavior of intermediaries useless. From an economic point of view, crypto-currencies are different from traditional currencies, and regulating them by thinking about traditional currencies, without distinguishing between them, is a mistake. Relying on history, operations and the economy of crypto-currencies, it may be seen that the legal system may adapt a cautious approach to its regulation, especially if it seeks restrictive objectives, such as protecting investors and consumers, or preventing commission of crimes. In this paper, therefore, suggestions of a cautious regulatory approach and with specific responses to remedy imminent problems are recommended. One may not have a clear idea of how crypto-currencies will interact with deliberative humans in this new way of generating and transferring wealth. So, to protect investors and consumers, or prevent the commission of crimes it is essential to adopt cautious regulatory approach and with specific responses to remedy imminent problems.

Crypto-currencies and other forms of digital money

Crypto-currencies are files, bits with data - such as the popular PDF or MP3 - that seek to fulfill all the functions assigned to traditional money, but using the internet as a means of transmission. Before delving into the concept, its economic conception and its legal categorization, it is useful to distinguish crypto-currencies from other similar concepts that invite confusion. In the order discussed, these are: i) digital money, ii) electronic money, iii) virtual currencies and, finally, iv) crypto-currencies.

Digital money or digital currency is the generic name for any intangible that is used as a means of digital payment. This should be understood as opposed to the concepts of physical money, metallic or paper money. Digital money is the genre that includes all the other categories: electronic money, virtual currencies and crypto-currencies (Arias and Sánchez, 2016 : 175-176; Simonetti Rojas, 2017; Tucker, 2009). The concept, although too broad to be legally categorized, is of interest to economists because it includes different means of payment that could have an impact on the general price level. Incipient studies in macroeconomics consider that digital money is a variable that should be considered in monetary theory, especially if it functions as a mechanism for the expansion of bank credit (Bjerg and others, 2017: 20-21; Fung, Molico and Stuber, 2014 ; Peters, Panayi and Chapelle, 2015).

Electronic money, also known as emoney, is an electronic means of payment that eventually "obliges in" or gives "the right to" money in current or circulating use and that bears its name (Khan, 2008 ; Rogers, 2005). The European Central Bank defines it as "an electronic deposit of monetary value [contained] in a technological device [software or hardware] that can be widely used to make payments to entities other than its issuer." [1] The United States has had legislation regulating electronic transactions and, therefore, electronic money since 1978 (Electronic Fund Transfer Act).

What distinguishes electronic money from other forms of digital money is that it requires a "contractual infrastructure" that assigns responsibilities between the parties and contains mechanisms to convert it into current money, even if these are not used in practice (Khan, 2008). The obligations generated by electronic money are analogous to those generated by transactions of documents representing money (Khan, 2008 ; Halaburda and Sarvary, 2016; Rogers, 2005: 1,257-1,262). With Paypal, for example, you can pay in dollars for a sale on the internet. But Paypal relies on credit cards and the contracts that support them and that assign responsibilities between the parties. This operation is not radically different from how a credit note or a check that is drawn against a checking account works. As Gans and Halaburda (2015) point out, electronic money is the "digital layer" of current money.

Virtual currencies are unregulated digital currencies that serve as a means of payment on the internet (European Central Bank, 2012: 13). It is important not to confuse them with representative commodity mechanisms. The latter would become the "digital layer" of money based on commodities (commodity money). Virtual currencies have their own denomination and have no correspondence in the physical world. They are not traded under the assumption that they are convertible into current money, even though secondary markets regularly allow such conversion (European Central Bank, 2012). Their usefulness as a means of payment - their main function - is determined by what can be purchased directly with them (Gans and Halaburda, 2015). Loyalty programs in flight miles are a type of virtual currency of growing popularity (European Central Bank, 2012; Castronova, 2014). Miles and virtual currencies are so similar when used as means of payment that many airlines are exploring transforming their miles into crypto-currencies.

Finally, crypto-currencies are a type of virtual currency with particular characteristics that allow them to have a universal and more widespread application. What makes them special is that they minimize the potential value problems associated with virtual worlds in which the same scarcity rules as the real world do not operate. They are also special because they work without intermediaries to validate transactions and, additionally, because in the most popular versions they are decentralized. Crypto-currencies are issued and change hands in a decentralized way using cryptography to maintain fidelity, in addition to registration technologies or accounting books that are maintained and updated by thousands of computers independently to verify that there are no duplicate uses (Brito and Castillo, 2013: 4 ; Halaburda and Sarvary, 2016: 2-3). Given these special characteristics, crypto-currencies aspire to have the same functions as electronic money and, therefore, current money (Halaburda and Sarvary, 2016: 5). They are what Makoto anticipated as the "logical but revolutionary next step in the history of money."

Before considering crypto-currencies technically, economically and legally, it is useful to review their History & Literature. Crypto-currencies are the last link in the evolution of virtual currencies, and knowing this evolutionary history allows one to understand their economic potential and limitations, as well as the challenges they present for legal science.

Literature Review: Evolution of virtual currencies

Crypto-currencies, which by design incorporate a scarcity that is not obvious in the virtual world, have the capacity to function as a means of payment and store of value without intermediaries or centralized repositories that consolidate, release and control payments in general, which makes it a revolutionary concept (Doguet, 2012 ; Jacobs, 2011 ; Nakamoto, 2009 ; Peters, Panayi and Chapelle, 2015). The headlines focused on their illegal uses, the massive hacks to intermediaries and their spectacular changes in value overshadow the dimension of this evolutionary leap (Kiviat, 2015: 571). Until the arrival of crypto-currencies, virtual currencies had never been able to transfer value detached from physical or virtual goods, nor had they had the virtue of being able to be managed autonomously. The significance of this leap is easier to understand in an evolutionary line in which computer games provide the most illustrative starting point.

The creation of virtual currencies

The circle of production and commercialization of digital wealth, which corresponds to the wealth that "supports" in an economic sense, was completed when exchange sites such as Ebay came into operations (Castronova, 2006 ; Shaviro, 2007). Unlike electronic money, virtual currencies were associated with platforms and are the real predecessors of crypto-currencies (Nazir, Hamilton and Tee, 2017). They are currencies without physical support and, therefore, without ties to the laws of physics and that, nevertheless, comply with essential economic characteristics of the physical support of current money: scarcity and rivalry (LeBlanc, 2016). Virtual currencies and crypto-currencies are scarce, they are rival goods that cannot be owned at the same time by two people, they do not have any support in the physical world and they derive their value from acceptance by users (Graf, 2014 : 55-58) .

Despite having existed for more than fifteen years, virtual currencies have not been a real threat to money in current use due to their limited circulation (European Central Bank, 2012). Some of them have reached sufficient levels of circulation to serve as a means of exchanging goods unrelated to the platforms that sustain them, prominently drugs and illegal goods (Filipkowski, 2008). The decision of the controllers to keep the virtual currencies linked to the platforms, together with their limited circulation, prevent them from becoming a medium of exchange, which is an essential function of the currency.

The problem of the exchange rate of virtual currencies

The purchasing power of a virtual currency outside the platform for which it was created is mainly subject to the price relationship between virtual goods within the platform and physical or virtual goods outside of it. This "exchange rate" is, in principle, analogous to the exchange rate between currencies that exists between countries. But in the case of countries, it is the market that determines, in most cases, the value at which the respective currencies are exchanged. This value responds to infinity of variables, such as the fiscal discipline of the countries in question, expectations of their economy and what can be bought today or tomorrow with the respective currencies.

The problem with virtual currencies is that the sovereign of one of the "countries" —the developer of the platform— absolutely controls the provision of goods within the platform and their prices: it can set prices of virtual goods as a supplier, it can change the marginal utility that these provide, and can, furthermore, produce them unlimitedly at very low marginal cost. This always exposes those who own these assets to relative devaluation that turns them into "risky assets".

The problem of control over virtual currencies

A second problem with platform-associated virtual currencies that limits their circulation is that they are centralized. This leaves the wealth of the parties - or their identity and property, at the mercy of a third party who mediates the transactions between them. Centralization, if it also includes the right to issue currency, allows virtual currencies to be subject to abusive seigniorage. The first problem is a problem with all electronic means of payment except crypto-currencies. The second is a particular problem with unsupported private currencies. Understanding each of these risks of centralization separately is useful to understand the evolutionary leap of crypto-currencies and why they are closer than other virtual currencies to paper money.

Centralization and the costs associated with the verification of transactions, plus the loss of formal anonymity that this entails, is inevitable in the transmission of electronic money. In the case of virtual currencies, a third party - usually the owner of the platform in the case of virtual currencies - has to register identities and transactions to prevent electronic or virtual currencies from being spent twice. This accounting or recording is not necessary in the case of a transaction involving physical money, because even a counterfeit bill cannot be used twice. But, as the early history of digital wealth shows, this is not obvious when it comes to digital files that are eminently copyable (Graf, 2014: 56). There is also a psychological incentive involved in maintaining this double counting in the case of virtual worlds (Shaviro, 2007). For two people to accept that they have actually entered into a digital transaction and spend time and work in obtaining the wealth that they then transfer in the virtual world, the balance that increases in the account of one regarding a transaction must decrease in the account of the other.

The centralization problem had seemed inevitable until the advent of crypto-currencies (Bonneau et al., 2015; Nakamoto, 2009). As Satoshi Nakamoto points out in the article with the conceptual foundations of Bitcoin, the permanent problem with electronic transactions is that they require a validator, since "the receiver cannot verify that the issuer has not spent the currency twice." This validator - as Nakamoto correctly pointed out - will always have factual power over the parties to an electronic transaction (Nakamoto, 2009). For example, he can refuse to make payments, reverse them, limit them to a certain amount, or use knowledge of the identity of the parties to favor one of them or himself. This is objectively a problem for all those who want to transact electronically with the security and anonymity equivalent to that afforded by a current money transaction between strangers.

Seigniorage over virtual currencies is potentially a more difficult problem to solve because the conflict of interest between users and the lord or issuer of the virtual currency is more direct. The developers of virtual currencies are not governed by legal institutions that give faith to all users that they will not change the rules or the exchange rates of their currencies or the amount of them circulating as central banks do. Virtual currencies are by definition unsupported and unregulated currencies. Of course, issuers could be contractually tied to the users of their platforms. They could declare that their currencies will follow a stable pattern. But like a dictator who controls the currency of a financially unstable country, the issuer of a virtual currency can always increase his seigniorage, which is the benefit of being the currency controller. The most obvious mechanisms at its disposal are to change the cost in time of using the currency versus holding it. For example, the loyalty program sponsors, such as flight mileage programs, are constantly accused of altering these factors by devaluing their currencies, which is the benefit of being the controller of the currency.

The operation and inherent advantages of crypto-currencies

The history and problems of virtual currencies allow us to understand why virtual currencies have given so much to talk about to academics. Crypto-currencies largely solve the problems of the dependence of the exchange rate on the demand for virtual goods because their price floats freely according to the demand. Likewise, crypto-currencies definitively solve the problem of centralization with the introduction of decentralized registration mechanisms that allow the parties to trade directly without any of the risks associated with the existence of intermediaries. The operation of Bitcoin and all the crypto-currencies that emulate it is tremendously complex. In a Bitcoin transaction, Alice sent from eWallet a file containing a private key encrypted data from a transaction, for example, a number of bitcoins to a known address or public key, contained in the electronic wallet of Bob's computer, which receives the transfer. (Dourado and Brito, 2014 ; Reid and Harrigan, 2011; Velde and others, 2013).

The private key sent by Alice to Bob, however, is a 34-character string - an alphanumeric string that's technically called a hash - derived from Alice's public address, which is also a 34-character string, and it recombines mathematically and encrypted to generate the transaction key. The operation Alice performs to generate the key that she sends to Bob is technically called "signing" the coin being transferred. Bob can only "see" in his wallet the bitcoins that Alice sent him because he received the private key that she sent him, that is, the bitcoins with Alice's signature in his wallet. The total bitcoins received by Bob make up a coin denominated in bitcoins. If Bob wants to spend the bitcoins received from Alice, then he must let wallet software to generate a new private key — this time derived from his public key in combination with the data of a new transaction. Only with that "signed" key can he resend the bitcoins. As each private key that is needed to transfer is derived cryptographically from the public key or address of the person transferring it, a reverse operation allows discovering all the public addresses through which a coin has passed. Thanks to this, and in this lies the essence of the mechanism, Bob - and in theory all users of the Bitcoin network - can check if Alice owned or had access to the bitcoins she sent to Bob in her wallet. (Dourado and Brito, 2014 ; Kroll, Davey and Felten, 2013 ; Velde and others, 2013). This design has several consequences that in theory matter to the law and that are worth anticipating.

Firstly, payments made in the Bitcoin network are irrevocable or they are understood to have been made since they were sent. Secondly, the sending of bitcoins is not reversible (Bonneau et al., 2015; Doguet, 2012 ; Kiviat, 2015 ; Lemieux, 2016 ;

Nakamoto, 2009 ; Simonetti Rojas, 2017 : 27). The receiver could do the reverse transaction, if the sender and receiver know each other and wish to do so. But direct trading between anonymous parties in Bitcoin is normally unconditional and one-way. Therefore, to subject transactions to conditions, it is necessary to schedule the shipment to a trustee (Bitcoin escrow) (Brito, Shadab and Castillo, 2015 : 206-208). Some crypto-currencies allow payment terms to be programmed into the same transfer and automatically verified, which is called a "smart contract" (Bonneau et al., 2015; McJohn and McJohn, 2016 ; Szabo, 1997).

The Bitcoin protocol and Blockchain explanations

A bitcoin transaction would be insecure if the transactions were simply sent from user to user. This is because while the cryptographic system can ensure that the sender sent the payment for a transaction that was valid given the previous transactions, there is nothing in the transactions themselves that prevents Alice from performing two transactions with Bob and Carol simultaneously in two transactions that separately would seem valid (Bonneau and others, 2015: 106). This is the double payment problem that Nakamoto refers to in the white paper that gave rise to Bitcoin. Double payment occurs because each coin itself can be traced to origin by each user individually, but no one can be sure that another user has not received it at the same time (Nakamoto, 2009). If to this is added the latency of the network, the result can be double payments or massive fraud (double-spending problem).

To solve the double payment problem, the Bitcoin protocol has a substantive rule and a procedural rule. The substantive rule states that only the first use of a currency is valid and all the others must be discarded as verified by the majority of the members of the user network. This redirects the problem to determining what the first use really is, and this is where the procedural rule comes into play. In a scenario where there is no centralized validator and, therefore, no single clock for all transactions (as would be the clock of the patent protection office), the absolute time does not serve as a parameter. Any transaction can be backdated, which opens up the possibility of infinite double-uses and fraud. The answer to this problem is an ordinal and chained record, that no one can control and that grows by consensus, and that tells the entire network what the chronological order of transactions has been since the transactions began.

This record, in the case of Bitcoin, is called the Blockchain and its mechanics are essential to understand why Bitcoin can work without intermediaries.

Blockchain operations are the result of a series of rules that coordinate the computers or nodes of the Bitcoin network and that seek to replace "democratically" a central authority that validates transactions. This ingenious system of collective consensus fixes the relative time of transactions and a technology that works. The Blockchain system grows by blocks or groups of transactions that are dated or ordinally stored in the block that contains them within the digital registry. The protocol only allows a block to be closed — if you prefer, to sign the sheet of a transaction log to close it — to specialized network users who are dedicated to solving mathematical problems with a high degree of randomness and that require a lot of computational power. 30These users are called "miners". Blocks are closed when a miner who proposed a block with pending transactions that are validatable succeeds in solving the required mathematical problem that "crystallizes" or "seals" the block. The miner who solves the block or closes the page of the book receives bitcoins as payment that the network itself generates by this process, hence the nickname "miner". Plus, you receive commissions for validated pending transactions. The consensus among miners on a closed block is verified when the miners decide to move to decipher a new problem to close the next block.

The work of choosing apparently valid transactions to propose a block and then competing to solve a mathematical problem to close it, the so-called "proof-of-work" that miners run, fulfills several functions in the Bitcoin network. Regarding the network, the proof of work and its payment in bitcoins generates incentives for miners to keep the chronological record of transactions and ensures that all individual transactions are quickly validated as soon as they are notified to the network (Kroll, Davey and Felten, 2013). This minimizes the problem of lag in the validation of transactions and, therefore, the problem of double payment. Today, for most users of the Bitcoin network, 50 minutes is enough to safely confirm that the received currency has not been used twice and can be used again.

Blockchain was the first distributed ledger or DLT (distributed, ledger technologies) or DAO (decentralized autonomous organization). There are hundreds of variations of DLT or DAO that emulate the operation of Blockchain for other uses (Maupin, 2017 ; Reyes, 2016). There have been many criticisms of the operation of Blockchain because its particular design has scalability problems (Croman and others, 2016) and because its transaction validation system is expensive in terms of the energy used by computers to solve the problems that allow to close a block and does not adjust to the entity of the transactions it processes. However, according to many, Blockchain, the first DLT, is the main computational innovation that brought Bitcoin to the world, an invention as revolutionary as the internet itself (Fenwick , Kaal and Vermeulen, 2017 : 363; Kiviat, 2015 : 573; Tapscott and Tapscott, 2016).

The Bitcoin network

Perhaps the least innovative but structurally essential is the user-to-user (peer-to-peer) network over which private keys are sent, public keys are kept, new transactions are announced, and new transactions are posted (Bonneau and others, 2015: 108). The network and its openness is vital to prevent transfer messages from being altered by a malicious group with excess computing power. Nodes in the Bitcoin network are randomly connected with at least eight outward connections, and up to 125 inward. Nodes in telephone connections do not receive connections from outside. To connect electronic wallets to users' computers for the first time, they connect to dedicated servers or seed nodes (Bonneau and others, 2015). There are wallet programs that download the entire Blockchain locally before initiating transactions and other wallet programs that trust the chains that are stored on third-party disks.

An economic generalization of crypto-currencies

From an economic point of view, the genius of crypto-currencies is not the fact that they can be traded without intermediaries or that they do not require faith (trustless) (Bonneau et al., 2015; Karlstrøm, 2014). Undoubtedly this is computationally revolutionary and a challenge for the existing legal institutions that regulate traditional currencies primarily through their intermediaries. Nor is it the fact that they are more portable, divisible, imperishable, practically un-forgeable, that they allow anonymity and have lower transaction costs, to mention some of the traditional attributions of currencies in which crypto-currencies excel. Economically, the genius of crypto-currencies lies in their ability to function with credible or predictable scarcity in an environment where scarcity is unnatural. Crypto-currencies have the ability to generate shortages of the money supply because their production is tied to the "proof of work" maintained by the same payment network, and because the latter is governed by adaptive mathematical challenges that require real effort and investment, but that are understandable by all users and are open to all who want to solve them. Bitcoin, in particular, owes its success to this predictability that was the incentive for its early adoption.

The backing of virtual currencies

Coins derive their usefulness from what can be bought with them and their purchasing power is based on the faith of those who receive it in payment of being able to use them again. Gold has not been used as currency for more than a century and it has not been used as currency backing for more than 80 years. Not even misnamed gold-backed virtual currencies like Goldcoin are actually currencies. Gold continues to be a safe asset for many people and, therefore, serves as a value store instrument (Barro and Misra, 2016).

But it ceased to be a unit of account and a medium of exchange, which are the other classical functions of money, because it was replaced by "better" currencies. His story serves to illustrate a popular theorem on the origin of the exchange value of money. It was Carl Menger, founder of the Austrian school, who suggested that a new currency's "usability" or its liquidity was what allowed it to prevail over other existing currencies. The triumph of a currency, Menger theorized, is recognized when the new currency begins to be the reference price for other goods (Davidson and Block, 2015).

Based on Menger's idea, Ludwig von Mises, another renowned Austrian school scholar, postulated that all existing currency arises from another currency, or if you prefer, inherits its exchange value from another currency and so on until it is reached some commodity used as currency for its value in use or intrinsic value (Davidson and Block, 2015 : 315-319). This theorem on the backing of currencies is known as the "Von Mises regression," and as such it emphasizes expectations, subjectivity, and the role of the price structure in substituting one currency for another (Rothbard, 1992; Selgin , 1994: 809-810). Gold is a commodity of intrinsic value as a jewel that became a currency, triumphed as such, then became an endorsement of more usable currencies to which it gave credibility, which in turn gave rise to many of the currencies currently in circulation. The US dollars and the Chilean peso fully comply with the Von Mises regression.

There are heated debates as to whether or not crypto-currencies like Bitcoin comply with the Von Mises regression, and if they do not, what would be their support. If Bitcoin does not have a use value like commodities and does not derive its value from another currency, and yet becomes a high-circulation currency or medium of exchange, they would defeat the hitherto unscathed regression of Von Mises (Davidson and Block, 2015). In this debate there are those who argue that Bitcoin would not challenge the theorem, because although it would not inherit its exchange value from any existing commodity or currency, it would have had some use value prior to becoming a medium of exchange (Graf, 2014). Its courage, its defenders say, could be justified as an attempt to support the libertarian cause. For the opponents, on the other hand, the question would be impertinent, since Bitcoin would not have enough circulation to be considered currency, which would make the theorem inapplicable (Yermack, 2015). The important thing about the theorem, these last authors emphasize, is that a currency must be heir to another currency in everything that implies the formation of expectations of being a unit of account and a medium of exchange.

Regardless of whether or not crypto-currencies meet the Von Mises regression, both parties are right on their basic premises. The exchange value of crypto-currencies is not derived from any traditional commodity. Bitcoin, for example, was created as a medium of exchange and appears to have been adopted de novo for its potential value as a medium of exchange (Graf, 2014). According to Graf, the proof of work executed by the miners who maintain the Blockchain, and the hardware and electricity they use to mine, cannot be considered backup, since the activity of mining bitcoins has no other use outside the Bitcoin network. As shown by various studies, Bitcoin and other crypto-currencies do not meet the condition of being a widely circulated medium of exchange and their denominations do not serve as a reference price for other goods due to their volatility (Bedecarratz, 2018 : 81; Lo and Wang , 2014 ; Spenkelink, 2014). Crypto-currencies are not only less liquid than gold and money: the total of them does not reach 1.9% of the value of world gold, nor do they cover 0.01% of world product in 2018.

Financially, crypto-currencies behave like an artificial commodity with a volatile price. Selgin (2015) trying to interfere with the debate, calls crypto-currencies "currencies derived from synthetic commodities" (synthetic commodity money). Assuming that bitcoins do not have the circulation required to challenge the Von Mises regression, the question that follows is how Bitcoin actually started to be traded. What was it that gave value change? The key to answering this question lies in an option that Satoshi Nakamoto took when creating Bitcoin. This decision guides the entire economic discussion about crypto-currencies and the need to regulate them.

The dilemma between retaining control of the currency or releasing it

Every creator of a virtual currency or a crypto-currency faces a dilemma when creating it: he can retain control of the money supply or he can abandon control of it. If you decide to stay in control, you have created a new form of virtual private money. In this case, you can benefit from being the lord or issuer of the currency, as explained in the section "The problem of control over virtual currencies." If you decide, on the other hand, to detach yourself from the control, you will have to obtain your usefulness as a user of it. The differences between the two options from an economic and legal point of view are radical.

Maintaining control of a private virtual currency involves triggering all the problems associated with the exchange rate and centralization reviewed above. It is difficult for a centralized virtual currency to generate enough consensus in the population to become a high-circulation medium of exchange. The problem is exacerbated by the potential for competition to emerge. No one would reasonably want to risk being expropriated by a currency controller, particularly if you have other more reliable currency alternatives that allow you to reserve money and exchange the goods you need. On the other hand, if the creator of a virtual currency decides to hand over control of the money supply to a system that does not depend on his will, he will not have the problem of exchange rates nor will he be able to take advantage of the power of centralization. This will have resolved a large part of the permanent suspicions that fall on virtual and non-virtual private money. But you will still have to encourage users to adopt your currency. To do this, it must offer a crypto-currency that is technologically superior and that, therefore, meets the conditions to overcome existing currencies in some or all forms of exchange where they reign (Halaburda and Sarvary, 2016: 29-30). But also, should provide an incentive to the first adopters to start circulation at their cost and support the infrastructure required for the currency to circulate before perceiving the network effects and the consequent increase in exchange value (Halaburda and Sarvary, 2016: 37- 41). The genius of Bitcoin is precisely in how its creator designed this incentive for early adoption.

From a monetary point of view, the activity of miners - the proof of work - predictably determines the autonomous growth of the supply of bitcoins, and that facilitated its adoption. You cannot add new bitcoins to the existing mass by buying them from someone. There is also no bank that issues bitcoins. There is no other way to create bitcoins other than by obtaining rewards for closing blocks. Every bitcoin that exists, or was mined by Nakamoto himself and other users when its cost was nonexistent or very low -because the problems to be solved were simple and required low processing capacity-, or it has been the result of miners' awards since mining became an economic activity. As Chris Ellis of Fathercoin points out in hindsight, for a crypto-currency to be successful the only truly essential ingredient is a community willing to accept it. It is speculated that the person or group of people who created Bitcoin under the pseudonym Satoshi Nakamoto are millionaires for having hoarded bitcoins anonymously when the cost of doing so was negligible (Champagne, 2018).

The dilemma between scalability and security of crypto-currencies

The issues outlined by Yermack and Roubini have been known to the crypto-currency community since its inception and have been debated. Roubini (2018) christened the problem the 'inconsistent trinity', following the ideas of one of the founders of a crypto-currency who tried to overcome the shortcomings of Bitcoin. This idea is referred to as the "Buterin Impossibility Theorem" for crypto-currencies, in honor of its original proponent. Vitalik Buterin, in a white paper that created Ethereum, a crypto-currency intended to overcome the rigidity of Bitcoin, pointed out that crypto-currencies could not have at the same time: i) scalability, that is, the possibility of adjusting the money supply quickly to maintain stable prices and to function as a medium of exchange; ii) decentralization, and iii) security. According to Buterin, you would always have to give up one of these characteristics in the design of a crypto-currency to obtain the other two. His theorem is sound when contrasted with the historical evidence we have for coins. Central banks offer scalability and security, but they are centralized and control the supply of currency. The decentralized systems of the existing currencies could have more flexibility and scalability, but at the cost of the security in the network that must be validating the transactions. This problem has been verified with new crypto-currencies like altcoins which, although more scalable in design than Bitcoin, are successfully attacked by miners of consolidated coins in what is called a 51% attack. If you want to have a secure and scalable system, you must retain centralization in some way. The latter was the bet of Ethereum and other crypto-currencies such as Peercoin. Its protocols, called "proof of interest" (proof-of-stake), give more weight in the consensus required to validate transactions to the user who has more interest in the destination of the currency, which implies a certain degree of centralization.

Centralized Block Chain

Finra R3 Research and their researcher Emily put forth a very valid document on Centralized Block Chain (Rutland, 2017). As per the research, a block chain can be either centralized or decentralized. It may be worth to note here, as per the research paper, that decentralized concept in this context may not be confused with distributed ledger principle in block chain and crypto-currencies. Whilst a block chain is inherently distributed, which means that many parties hold copies of the ledger, it is not inherently decentralized. So, though a block chain is centralized or decentralized, it essentially refers to right of participants on the ledger. Thus, in essence, it is merely a question of design. Within the decentralized network, anyone may participate and transact on the ledger. So, a mechanism needs to be in existence so as to combat the vulnerabilities, which arise from this design to assure that transactions are legitimate. Bitcoin, for instance, is decentralized block chain that makes use of mining and proof-of-work to ensure integrity of ledger and prevents corrupting the system.

A centralized network, which can be a better way in many respects, comprises only of parties whose identities are known. So anyone, unlike in decentralized block chain, cannot just join the network and leads into a system that has better validity as only credible and reputable participants may post to the ledger. Since the network participants identities are known, so their transactions can also be audited. Furthermore, centralized distributed ledger has its right potential to be used in the regulated industries like in BFSI Domain industries and financial services. This will help to minimize vulnerabilities. Whilst both decentralized and centralized block chains may still have related risks, but centralized networks are preferred for the purpose in that the identity of participants is verified. Consequently, audit trail does exist, should an actor attempts to tamper the systems. It may be worth noting here that participants, including the founders, may not be verifiable as some even bear the pseudonyms. One never knows that how the things take shape in the future and some unanticipated risk warrants the need of an accurate identity (Rutland, 2017).

Thus, in financial domain, it is always preferable, for example, to deal with the known entity that enters into a valid transaction rather than being a party to an account where every possible manipulation that could potentially occur in an anonymous, decentralized network. Although, Proof-of-work (PoW) exists, which is a function to prevent attacks and other cybercrimes on decentralized network by needing some level of work that is usually costly and time consuming, but it cannot prevent all sort of attacks. For example, PoW protocol resolves double-spending problem, but, if a hacker has access to hash power more than half of total hash power then the hacker can still launch a double-spending attack or 51% attack. This cost of creation of 51% attack can be potentially low if hash power is abundantly available. This can then be an extensive risks to decentralized networks, like PoW block chains (Yang, Chen, & Chen, 2019).

If the third world countries like India, wish to use Bloch Chain and crypto-currencies then it is required to have a careful choice of using a better technology for e-Governance. Bringing in Block chain in e-governance and usage of crypto-currencies can be inevitable. For example, bringing in this new disruptive technology can be necessary in BFSI Domains as well as in other domains like land records and agriculture. This will not only bring efficiency and transparency, but, will also put a check on frauds. India, for instance saw a series of frauds like the one committed by Nirav Modi, Choksi, and others. Block Chain can put an effective check, but, the technologies like Centralized Block Chains can be useful as the network would be participated from the people having known identity. Though no one can say that Block chain can put a stopper to all frauds, but, at least it can arrest the growth of frauds.

A legal generalization of crypto-currencies

The state of the art of the study of crypto-currencies in the area of law is primary and less than that observed in areas such as science and economics. The situation is understandable. This is an entirely new situation for which positive law has few answers. With electronic money, it was easy to adapt the existing categories and concepts, since the parts and content of the obligations, and in general everything that concerns the law, remained practically unchanged (Khan, 2008 ; Rogers, 2005). In addition, the regulation of electronic money had obvious recipients that were already subject to regulation: the banks and financial intermediaries that took most of the burden of legal innovations in the matter.

With crypto-currencies, on the other hand, the existing legal categories and concepts, from those applicable to the definition of wealth or property, to tradition, to intermediaries, to the intervention of force and others, are difficult to extend and do not work well in virtual environments that serve as antecedent and sustenance (Bartle, 2004 ; Graf, 2015). The problems derived from the self-execution of contracts, the irreversibility of transactions and the existence of anonymous parties, among others, are all aspects in which positive law appears irremediably exceeded. In Indian context, with reference to the Laws of Contract, the parties must be competent and specific in order to enter into a contract. In case of decentralized network, if the parties are working anonymously and enter in a smart contract, then such terms of contract cannot be validated by an Indian Court of Law or Indian Judicial system. For example, if a minor enters into a contract, then this contract shall be null and void (Upadhyay, 2014). Thus, the proposition is to make suitable amendments in Law such that these type of exceptions can be considered legal, which looks to be a remote possibility. The best solution, therefore, is to adopt suitable block chain technology and a crypto based on a suitable block chain.

Cryptom

A new crypto currency is being proposed, coined as "Cryptom". This currency would be founded on a a centralized Block Chain. Such technology would work with parties that are specific and competent as well as empowered or nominated to act in their specific roles. The parties who can enter the network cannot be anonymous and shall be of verifiable identity. Thus, if they enter into some contract, the terms of the contract can be valid in the eyes of Law, as per the Laws of Contract specifications. The details of the currency, its source code and

What kind of good are crypto-currencies? The problem of legal nature

According to Pérez Abarca and Simonetti Rojas, bitcoins in Chile would be a not forbidden thing, therefore, an object of human commerce. Discussing what it would be and given that bitcoins are not sanctioned as money by the Chilean State, Pérez Abarca (2015 : 78-80) declares them "currencies", which coincides with European international jurisprudence. Simonetti Rojas (2017 : 38), on the other hand, following North American jurisprudence, calls them «digital movable property». The latter is equivalent to declaring them digital commodities that can be used as a means of payment. To these positions can be added that of Bedecarratz (2018: 82), which declares them a sui generis intangible good that behaves economically in a similar way to a commodity. Pérez Abarca and Bedecarratz do not justify their position in Chilean positive law. For Simonetti Rojas, given that the definition of the Chilean Central Bank, like that of the US Supreme Court (Mandjee, 2014), requires that a "currency" be legal money from another country and Bitcoin is not in any country, it could not be qualified as such. In any case, Pérez Abarca and Simonetti Rojas agree that the legal figure applicable in Chile to a transaction that involves a payment in bitcoins would be the barter rules and those that regulate the sale in subsidy.

To begin with, it should be noted that if someone wanted to formally defeat each of these definitions, they could point out that the Chilean Central Bank calls money issued by recognized governments currencies and that, therefore, crypto-currencies cannot be currencies, as Pérez Abarca points out. . But it could also say that the Civil Code establishes that assets consist of corporeal and intangible things (Article 565), and that corporeal - which have a real being that can be perceived - are divided into movable or immovable, the former having the characteristics that they are transportable (article 567). According to these definitions, bitcoins could not be a commodity or a "digital movable good" as Simonetti Rojas points out. Finally, they could not be an intangible good either, since these are real rights that one has over things and that all third parties must respect, or personal rights, that one has against certain third parties (Article 576). Therefore, none of the three existing definitions would survive a formalist attack. The fact that Bedecarratz calls crypto-currencies sui generis intangible assets only confirms the difficulty of extending the existing legal categories in the Civil Code to crypto-currencies.

Determining the legal nature of crypto-currencies generates innumerable consequences in the legal framework. This ranges from who should regulate them or how they are taxed, to what are the obligations for the parties that a crypto-currency transaction generates. No legislation of advanced nations has comprehensively and directly regulated the phenomenon of crypto-currencies. What motivated the European jurisprudence regarding crypto-currencies was an attached question about whether the brokerage service - the commission of the seller of crypto-currencies in euros - should pay the value added tax. 46For its part, what has motivated North American jurisprudence is mostly cases in which it is suspected that crypto-currencies have been used to launder money. In these cases, open figures designed to capture this last phenomenon are applied, and it is limited to identifying crypto-currencies as a security suitable for money laundering. There are also scattered norms that regulate obligations such as the one that requires financial intermediaries to save their clients' data to improve the traceability of operations. Even in Asia, where these are most popular, regulation is limited to financial aspects, such as risk exposure and reporting obligations of intermediaries. 47

Leaving aside the formalism and accepting that crypto-currencies are an unnamed good that can be the object of human commerce or a crypto-asset, the right of obligations also appears as limited. According to the aforementioned authors, the swap would be the applicable legal figure. But this fails when it is technically verified in the way described in the section "Crypto-currency transactions".

How do you trade crypto-currencies? The problem of law in contracts

The swap is one of the most flexible figures in the continental legal system when things that are not money are exchanged. At its base are basic legal institutions such as surrender, possession, and dominance. When it comes to bitcoins, the material delivery would occur by revealing the sequence of numbers that entitles the bitcoins and the tradition would occur - if the term is applicable - at this very moment, as it would give the new user the right to use them immediately . As it is an asset subject to registration, following the general principles, the domain by "purchasing confirmation" would be acquired after several blocks have been added to the chain and the operation is confirmed by most of the nodes in the network.

There are, however, several problems when analyzing potential conflicts between the parties in this very simple operation. First, since there is a time between the transaction and it being written in stone in blocks of the registry chain that prevents dual use, payment in crypto-currencies, if accepted as it is apparently accepted in Japan, would not be an "effective payment." . In other words, crypto-currencies would allow "physical" double possession that is not simply a duplicate registration. The additional complication here is that there is no contract with any issuer, not even with the Bitcoin foundation in charge of promoting the technology, to discard one operation or prefer the other or to correct the record. A user could reveal the private keys without intention to transfer the domain and transfer it,48 It should be remembered that according to the substantive standard of the Bitcoin protocol, the first transaction must be validated, regardless of the conditions in which it occurred. It is technically impossible to ask each node on the network to verify whether the history of each transaction is legitimate. This is contrary to what traditional law commands. Blockchain, if it is proof of something, it is of possession, regardless of whether it is legitimate or illegitimate (Graf, 2015). In the Bitcoin network there are no stolen bitcoins, because in its design there can be no third parties with the possibility of controlling transactions or reversing them. The way they are dealt with makes the figure of theft, and in general the cause and the object in terms of the Civil Code, irrelevant.

Simple trade-in problems don't end with the issue of delivery, possession, or cause. If the thief of bitcoins or who has received them could be known and should not receive them, a judge would have no way to force their holder to return them. Access to the alphanumeric sequence to transfer a currency is not a personal right or a credit, because there is no one against whom to exercise it (Graf, 2014 : 59). Therefore, there is no way to seize bitcoins. 49Unless the authority gains access to the computer or the private keys that entitle them or tortures the possessor to reveal the sequences, it will not be able to seize. Bitcoins could exist as sequences only in the thief's mind and there they would be untouchable. The alternative would be to force it into alternative compliance. The inconsistency in this option is that the judge would be forcing to return an asset that the thief still owns simply because he has no way to force it to return it. There have already been cases of divorce in England in which one of the parties protected their assets in bitcoins. fifty

Traditional institutions, real property law - which contains the definition of thing - and derivative institutions such as possession and tradition, or enforcement, do not seem easily applicable to crypto-currencies. As Graf points out,

bureaucratic classificationism that insists that all activities can fall within a limited set of expandable categories defined by the legislator has been powerful in history [...] In the case of Bitcoin it takes the form of attempts to call Bitcoin illegal because it is not It fits into any of the existing categories or constructs (Graf, 2015).

So far, existing legal works tend to avoid the tedious task of defining the legal nature of crypto-currencies. It is easier to resort to the legal definition of money to rule out that crypto-currencies are, or to try to see what the people who have them do, if they use them as a means of payment or investment, to see if they should be regulated by central banks , the agencies that protect private investments, those that control the exchange of international currencies, the law of contracts, or to escape the regulation of all of them, among other possibilities (Grinberg, 2012: 194; Haesly, 2016 ; Kaplanov, 2012 : 150; Litwack, 2015 : 310; Walch, 2016). As the simple example of the swap shows, all these approaches will be unsatisfactory to the extent that we do not ask ourselves the legal questions in the correct order by putting the person at the center of the analysis, as suggested by Graf (2015).

A regulatory approach to crypto-currencies

Positive law has few current answers to face the phenomenon of crypto-currencies and it is risky to try to insert new regulations in local legal systems without being clear about their legal nature and without the language having chosen enough to precisely regulate the phenomenon. (Walch, 2016). There is also the additional risk that premature imprecise regulatory attempts will inhibit parallel technological developments that are related to technology; for example, Blockchain developments (Kiviat, 2015).

Notwithstanding these objections, their own functioning and the economy that supports them give clues as to how a "regulatory fence" could begin to be developed around these technologies that allows solving imminent problems and comprehensively regulating them when justified and possible. done effectively.

The first thing to note is that the threat of local regulation has an impact on adoption, despite the fact that traditional regulatory tools appear technically inept. The current money price of crypto-currencies reacts positively or negatively to news in which it is announced that they could be prohibited or accepted in some relevant economies (Auer and Claessens, 2018). Some reasons that could explain this is that the news affects expectations. For example, the news of increased interoperability with banks and financial institutions has positive impacts on the current price of crypto-currencies (Auer and Claessens, 2018). On the contrary, the prohibitions, even if they are not effective, limit the circulation capacity of crypto-currencies, especially among less advanced or risk-averse users.

In general, there are three main areas that are used to justify a restrictive regulation of crypto-currencies: avoiding illegal activities, protecting consumers and investors, and protecting financial stability and the payment system (Auer and Claessens, 2018 ; Puvogel Rojas, 2018) . As I pointed out in the sections "The Dilemma Between Facilitating Early Adoption and Price Stability" and "The Dilemma Between Scalability and Security of Crypto-currencies," given their limited circulation and technological barriers to overcoming scalability and security issues. , there are no threats to financial stability and the payment system. This has been done to see various reports of the Bank for International Settlements (BPI,2018). I will therefore focus on the first two objectives.

The first approach to the phenomenon should be to distinguish what type of currency you are trying to regulate. As noted in the chapter "An Economic Generalization of Crypto-currencies", crypto-currencies have very different ways of dealing with the problem of endorsement and early adoption, giving rise to crypto-currencies of a different nature. Following the distinctions made in that section, regulation should be very different in the case of centralized or backed crypto-currencies than in the case of decentralized, programmed scarcity - or unsupported - currencies such as Bitcoin. In the case of the former, regulation should be less intense or intrusive because the very mechanics with which they operate allows traditional law to be more effective. As a general rule,51

The most complex case is that of decentralized and unsupported crypto-currencies that are maintained with technologies without trust (trustless) such as Blockchain and in which there is quasi-anonymity, especially when they are regulated for restrictive reasons, such as consumer protection, investor protection or to avoid illicit.

The main problem with regulation in this case is that the aims are clear but the existing tools are weak, which allows recipients to decide to fall outside or within it. For example, if the fear is that Bitcoin is being used to finance or pay for what Foley, Karlsen and Putniņš (2018) call black e-commerce, which accounted for 25% of crypto-currency transactions by 2018, the risk of prohibition is to inhibit 75% of legal activities. 52 That is why the «blacklists» of bitcoin addresses involved in illegal transactions as a means of preventing crimes, as has been proposed (Bedecarratz, 2018), can be ineffective for the purpose.

For all of the above, an approach to the phenomenon of crypto-currencies, especially decentralized ones and without support, should be one that obeys expansive reasons, that invites the generation of points of contact with the existing legal system and that normalizes its use. The idea is to get more users to adopt currencies and give them traceability and more public attention. This will not prevent the crime. Whoever wants to commit crimes or defraud consumers or investors can do so from more opaque currencies. This behavior is precisely what some authors found (Auer and Claessens, 2018). The levels of illegal transactions in Bitcoin were decreasing as this system gained more public attention.

The possible actions to implement this strategy are varied. For example, allowing them to be purchased with credit cards, which are recognized as an investment instrument, that issuers are invited to register and make transparent usage figures and their money supply formulas, that profits and losses are allowed to be taxed, and discounting costs - something that is already implemented in Chile according to Official Letter 963-2018 of the Internal Revenue Service -, that exchanges or intermediaries are authorized and keep records of their clients - an approach known as know your client -, among others (Gamble , 2017 : 352; Mandjee, 2014 : 34-38; Maupin, 2017 : 5-6; Ven, 2018 : 20).

These measures, which do not comprehensively regulate the phenomenon, are not incompatible with the discussion in courts of problems that occur in transactions with crypto-currencies and with the ex post active prosecution of fraud against investors and consumers, and of all crimes by the media. that the law allows in court. The courts have a very important role in raising the questions that the legal system must answer when we are in a position to have a comprehensive and permanent regulation of this new technology. It is not about building a regulation based on national and foreign judicial decisions, which can be doctrinally very deficient, but about raising the questions that the legal system must answer. The concern of trying a comprehensive regulation and for restrictive reasons,

CONCLUSION

In the face of such important gaps in positive law, it is inevitable to suggest the obvious. A new approach, new rules and institutions are needed to be able to correctly capture what users do with crypto-currencies. So far, however, it is not necessary to do it fully. The risk of regulating by inhibiting disruptive innovation is high, and the gains from doing so are low. It seems a better strategy to limit yourself to trying to avoid illegal uses and prosecute imminent abuses as other jurisdictions do, and to try to normalize the use of crypto-currencies by facilitating their interaction with the legal system, especially in cases of consolidated crypto-currencies. Just as you cannot collect personal taxes in economies with a high degree of informality,

The best approach for the moment is therefore to wait. See how the conflicts between parties that transact in crypto-currencies in courts are evolving. The courts, which function in a decentralized manner and extending existing norms to supervening events, have the ability to collect cross-sectional information on potential conflicts such as those I described in the previous section regarding the exchange and forced execution, or to determine the criminal operation in the crypto-currencies that are wrapped. With a few years of conflict and the questions they bring, we may be in a position to understand what problems crypto-currency transactions cause real people in real transactions, and design regulation that puts them at the center. After all,

BIBLIOGRAPHIC REFERENCES

Álvarez, A., Bignon, V. (2013). "L. Walras and C. Menger: Two ways on the path of modern monetary theory". European Journal of the History of Economic Thought. 20 (1), 89-124. Recovered from http://doi.org/10.1080/09672567.2011.596939 [Links]

Ametrano, F. (2016). "Bitcoin, Blockchain, and distributed ledgers: Between hype and reality". SSRN Electronic Journal. . Recovered from http://doi.org/10.2139/ssrn.2832249 [Links]

Ametrano, F. (2016). "Hayek money: The crypto-currency price stability solution". SSRN Electronic Journal. . Recovered from http://doi.org/10.2139/ssrn.2425270 [Links]

Arias, G., Sánchez, A. (2016). "The digital currency challenge for the regulatory regime". Chilean Journal of Law and Technology. 5 (2), 173-209. Recovered from http://doi.org/10.5354/0719-2584.2016.43541 [Links]

Auer, R., Claessens, S. (2018). Regulation of crypto-currencies: Evaluation of market reactions . BPI. Recovered from https://bit.ly/2TZktpy [Links]

Babaioff, M., Dobzinski, S., Oren, S., Zohar, A. (2012). On Bitcoin and red balloons . Recovered from http://doi.org/10.1145/2229012.2229022 [Links]

European Central Bank,., (2012). Virtual currency schemes . Frankfurt am Main: European Central Bank [Links]

Barber, A. (2015). "Bitcoin and the philosophy of money: Evaluating the commodity status of digital currencies". Spectra. 4 (2). Retrieved from http: // http: //doi.org/10.21061/spectra.v4i2.241 [Links]

Barro, R., Misra, S. (2016). "Gold returns". The Economic Journal. 126 (594), 1293-1317.

Recovered from http://doi.org/10.1111/ecoj.12274 [Links]

Bartle, R. (2004). Pitfalls of virtual property . Recovered from http://bit.ly/2IoSH0Y [Links]

Bedecarratz, F. (2018). "Criminal risks of virtual currencies". Chilean Journal of Law and Technology. 7 (1), 79-105. Recovered from http://doi.org/10.5354/0719-2584.2018.48515 [Links]

Bjerg, O., McCann, D., Macfarlane, L., Hougaard Nielsen, R., Ryan-Collins, J., (2017). Seigniorage in the 21st Century: A study of the profits from money creation in the United Kingdom and Denmark . Frederiksberg: Copenhagen Business School [Links]

Blundell-Wignall, A. (2014). The Bitcoin question: Currency versus trust-less transfer technology . Recovered from http://doi.org/10.1787/20797117 [Links]

Böhme, R., Christin, N., Edelman, B., Moore, T. (2015). "Bitcoin: Economics, technology, and governance". The Journal of Economic Perspectives. 29 (2), 213-238. Recovered from http://doi.org/10.1257/jep.29.2.213 [Links]

Bonneau, J., Miller, A., Clark, J., Narayanan, A., Kroll, J., Felten, E. (undated). SoK: Research perspectives and challenges for Bitcoin and crypto-currencies . In 2015 IEEE Symposium on Security and Privacy. (104-121). Recovered from http://doi.org/10.1109/SP.2015.14 [Links]

BPI, B. (no date). Crypto-currencies: Beyond the trendy phenomenon . Recovered from http://bit.ly/2Ilkqjj [Links]

Brito, J., Castillo, A., (2013). Bitcoin: A primer for policymakers . Arlington: Mercatus Center at George Mason University [Links]

Brito, J., Shadab, H., Castillo, A. (2015). "Bitcoin financial regulation: Securities, derivatives, prediction markets, and gambling". Columbia Science and Technology Law Review. . Recovered from http://doi.org/10.2139/ssrn.2423461 [Links]

Castronova, E. (2001). "Virtual worlds: A first-hand account of market and society on the cyberian frontier". CESifo Working Paper Series. 618 . Recovered from http://bit.ly/2Ik0Io2 [Links]

Castronova, E. (2006). "A cost-benefit analysis of real-money trade in the products of synthetic economies". Info. 8 (6), 51-68. Recovered from http://doi.org/10.1108/14636690610707482 [Links]

Castronova, E., (2014). Wildcat currency . New Haven: Yale University Press [Links]

Chaum, D. (1992). "Achieving electronic privacy". Scientific American. 267 (2), 96-101. Recovered

from
http://doi.org/10.1038/scientificamerican0892-96 [Links]

Cline, E., (2011). Ready player one . Portland: Broadway Books [Links]

Croman, K., Decker, C., Eyal, I., Gencer, A., Juels, A., Kosba, A., Miller, A., Saxena, P., Shi, E., Gün Sirer, E. , SonRoger Wattenhofer, D. (2016). On scaling decentralized blockchains . In Clark, J., Meiklejohn, S., Ryan, P., Wallach, D., Brenner, M., Rohloff, K (eds.); Financial cryptography and data security: FC 2016. Lecture notes in computer science. (106-125). Berlin: Springer Recovered from http://doi.org/10.1007/978-3-662-53357-4_8 [Links]

Davidson, L., Block, W. (2015). "Bitcoin, the Regression Theorem, and the emergence of a new medium of exchange". The Quarterly Journal of Austrian Economics. 18 (3), 311-338. Recovered from http://bit.ly/2HZ9uJf [Links]

Doguet, J. (2012). "The nature of the form: Legal and regulatory issues surrounding the Bitcoin digital currency system". Louisiana Law Review. 73 (4), 1118-1153. Recovered from http://bit.ly/2HYyIHF [Links]

Dourado, E., Brito, J. (2014). Crypto-currency . In The New Palgrave Dictionary of Economics. (1-9). London: Palgrave Macmillan [Links]

Dwyer, G. (2015). "The economics of Bitcoin and similar private digital currencies". Journal of Financial Stability. 17 , 81-91. Recovered from http://doi.org/10.1016/j.jfs.2014.11.006 [Links]

Fenwick, M., Kaal, W., Vermeulen, E. (2017). "Legal education in the Blockchain revolution". Vanderbilt Journal of Entertainment & Technology Law. 20 (2), 351-383. Recovered from http://bit.ly/2HXHc1A [Links]

Filipkowski, W. (2008). "Cyber laundering: An analysis of typology and techniques". International Journal of Criminal Justice Sciences. 3 (1), 15-27. Recovered from http://doi.org/10.2139/ssrn.2939127 [Links]

Foley, S., Karlsen, J., Putniņš, T. (2018). "Sex, drugs, and Bitcoin: How much illegal activity is financed through crypto-currencies?". The Review of Financial Studies. 32 (5), 1798-1853. Recovered from http://doi.org/10.1093/rfs/hhz015 [Links]

Fung, B., Molico, M., Stuber, G. (2014). Electronic money and payments: Recent developments and issues . Recovered from http://bit.ly/2HX9dqc [Links]

Gamble, C. (2017). "The legality and regulatory challenges of decentralized crypto-currency: A Western perspective". International Trade and Business Review. 20 . [Links]

Gans, J., Halaburda, H. (2015). Some economics of private digital currency . In Goldfarb, A., Greenstein, S., Tucker, C (eds.); Economic analysis of the digital economy. (257-276). Oxford: Oxford University Press Retrieved from http://doi.org/10.7208/chicago/9780226206981.003.0009 [Links]

Graf, K. (2014). "Commodity, scarcity, and monetary value theory in light of bitcoin". Prices & Markets. 3 (3), 1-24. Recovered from http://bit.ly/2HY84hZ [Links]

Graf, K., (2015). Are Bitcoins ownable ?: Property rights, IP wrongs, and legal-theory implications . [Links]

Grinberg, R. (2015). "Bitcoin: An innovative alternative digital currency". Hastings Science & Technology Law Journal. 4 (1), 159-208. Recovered from http://bit.ly/2HVwfgR [Links]

Haesly, K. (2016). "How to solve a problem like Venezuela: An argument for virtual currency". Law and Business Review of the Americas. 22 (3), 261-270. Recovered from http://bit.ly/2HXl1bJ [Links]

Halaburda, H., Sarvary, M., (2016). Beyond bitcoin: The economics of digital currencies . Basingstoke: Palgrave Macmillan [Links]

Heeks, R. (2009). "Understanding" gold farming "and real-money trading as the intersection of real and virtual economies". Journal for Virtual Worlds Research. 2 (4), 4-27. Recovered from http://doi.org/10.4101/jvwr.v2i4.868 [Links]

Iwamura, M., Kitamura, Y., Matsumoto, T., Saito, K. (2014). "Can we stabilize the price of a crypto-currency ?: Understanding the design of Bitcoin and its potential to compete with Central Bank money". SSRN Electronic Journal. , 1-39. Recovered from http://doi.org/10.2139/ssrn.2519367 [Links]

Jacobs, E. (2011). "Bitcoin: A bit too far?". Journal of Internet Banking and Commerce. 16 (2). Recovered from http://bit.ly/2wDBHij [Links]

Kaplanov, N. (2012). "Nerdy money: Bitcoin, the private digital currency, and the case against its regulation." Loyola Consumer Law Review. 25 (1), 111-174. Recovered from http://bit.ly/2wFmr4u [Links]

Karlstrøm, H. (2014). "Do libertarians dream of electric coins? The material embeddedness of Bitcoin". Distinktion: Journal of Social Theory. 15 (1), 23-36. Recovered from http://doi.org/10.1080/1600910X.2013.870083 [Links]

Khan, A. (2008). "A theoretical analysis of payment systems". South Carolina Law Review. 60 (2), 1-66. Recovered from http://bit.ly/2wDCCzh [Links]

Kiviat, T. (2015). "Beyond Bitcoin: Issues in regulating Blockchain transactions". Duke Law Journal. 65 , 569-608. Recovered from http://bit.ly/2wFUKbv [Links]

Kroll, J., Davey, I., Felten, E. (2013). The economics of Bitcoin mining or, Bitcoin in the presence of adversaries . In The Twelfth Workshop on the Economics of Information Security. (11-32). Washington DC [Links]

Lastowka, G., Hunter, D. (2004). "The laws of the virtual worlds". California Law Review. 92 (1), 1-74. Recovered from http://doi.org/10.15779/Z386H7P [Links]

LeBlanc, G. (2016). The effects of crypto-currencies on the banking industry and monetary policy Eastern Michigan University, Open Access Senior Honors, Michigan Retrieved from http://bit.ly/2MtROJX [Links]

Lemieux, V. (2016). "Trusting records: Is Blockchain technology the answer?". Records Management Journal. 26 (2), 110-139. Recovered from http://doi.org/10.1108/RMJ-12-2015-0042 [Links]

Litwack, S. (2015). "Bitcoin: Currency or fool's gold: A comparative analysis of the legal classification of Bitcoin notes & comments". Temple International & Comparative Law Journal. 29 (2). Recovered from http://bit.ly/2Iop67P [Links]

Lo, S., Wang, C. (2014). "Bitcoin as money?" Current Policy Perspectives. 14 (4). Recovered from http://bit.ly/2wEyqiE [Links]

Mandjee, T. (2014). "Bitcoin, its legal classification and its regulatory framework". Journal of Business and Securities Law. 15 (2), 157-218. Recovered from http://bit.ly/2wEyWNC [Links]

Maupin, J. (2017). "Mapping the global legal landscape of Blockchain and other executive

summary: Distributed ledger technologies". CIGI
Academic Paper Series. . Retrieved from
http://bit.ly/2wBhCsK [Links]

McJohn, S., McJohn, I. (2016). "The Commercial
Law of Bitcoin and Blockchain transactions".
Uniform Commercial Code Law Journal. . Recovered
from http://bit.ly/2wEIRCG [Links]

Nakamoto, S. (2009). Bitcoin: A peer-to-peer
electronic cash system Bitcoin: A Peer-to-Peer
Electronic Cash System . Bitcoin.org. Recovered
from https://bitcoin.org/en/bitcoin-paper [Links]

Nazir, M., Hamilton, J., Tee, S. (2017). "Real money
trading in virtual worlds". Proceedings of the 17th
International Conference on Electronic Business. .
Recovered from http://bit.ly/2KtsSzD [Links]

Peach, T. (2009). "Adam Smith and the labor theory
of (real) value: A reconsideration". History of
Political Economy. 41 (2), 383-406. Recovered from

http://doi.org/10.1215/00182702-2009-007 [Links]

Pérez Abarca, R. (2015). The legal regime of the permutation contract in jurisprudence (Bachelor of Legal and Social Sciences). University of Chile, Faculty of Law, Santiago, Chile. Recovered from http://bit.ly/2WOMWTy [Links]

Peters, G., Panayi, E., Chapelle, A. (2015). "Trends in crypto-currencies and blockchain technologies: A monetary theory and regulation perspective". Journal of Financial Perspectives. 3 (3), 92-113. Recovered from http://bit.ly/2wFi614 [Links]

Puvogel Rojas, M. (2018). Blockchain and virtual currencies: A legal approach (Bachelor of Legal and Social Sciences). University of Chile, Faculty of Law, Santiago, Chile. Recovered from http://bit.ly/2wEBsDy [Links]

Reid, F., Harrigan, M. (undated). An analysis of anonymity in the Bitcoin system . In 2011 IEEE Third

International Conference on Privacy, Security, Risk and Trust and 2011 IEEE Third International Conference on Social Computing. (1318-1326). Recovered from http://bit.ly/2wzZgbJ [Links]

Reyes, C. (2016). "Moving beyond Bitcoin to an endogenous theory of decentralized ledger technology regulation: An initial proposal". Villanova Law Review. 61 (1), 191-234. Recovered from http://bit.ly/2Xt8H8H [Links]

Rogers, J. (2005). "The new old law of electronic money". Southern Methodist University Law Review. 58 (4), 1253-1312. Recovered from http://bit.ly/2XzrdfK [Links]

Rothbard, M., (1992). The gold standard: Perspectives in the Austrian school . Auburn: Ludwig von Mises Institute [Links]

Roubini, N. (2018). Crypto is the mother of all scams and (now busted) bubbles while Blockchain is the most over-hyped technology ever, no better than a spreadsheet / database . [Links]

Selgin, G. (1994). "On ensuring the acceptability of a new fiat money". Journal of Money, Credit and Banking. 26 (4), 808-826. Recovered from http://doi.org/10.2307/2077948 [Links]

Selgin, G. (2015). "Synthetic commodity money". Journal of Financial Stability. 17 , 92-99. Recovered from http://doi.org/10.1016/j.jfs.2014.07.002 [Links]

Shaviro, S. (2007). Money for Nothing: Virtual Worlds and Virtual Economies . Recovered from http://bit.ly/2EUz2VQ [Links]

Shin, D. (2008). "Understanding purchasing behaviors in a virtual economy: Consumer behavior involving virtual currency in Web 2.0 communities". Interacting with Computers. 20 (4-5), 43-446. Recovered from http://doi.org/10.1016/S0953-5438(08)00025-8 [Links]

Simonetti Rojas, J. (2017). Concept and legal nature of crypto-currencies (Bachelor of Legal Sciences). Pontificia Universidad Católica de Valparaíso, Faculty of Law, Santiago, Chile. [Links]

Smith, A., (1794). Investigation of the nature and causes of the wealth of nations . Valladolid [Links]

Spenkelink, H. (2014). The adoption process of crypto-currencies: Identifying factors that influence the adoption of crypto-currencies from a multiple stakeholder perspective (master in Industrial Engineering and Management). University of Twente, Twente, The Netherlands. [Links]

Szabo, N. (1997). "Formalizing and securing relationships on public networks". First Monday. 2 (9). Recovered from http://bit.ly/2Xw0cK2 [Links]

Tapscott, D., Tapscott, A., (2016). Blockchain revolution: How the technology behind Bitcoin is changing money, business, and the world . New York: Penguin [Links]

Task Force on Stored-Value Cards. (1996). "A commercial lawyer's take on the electronic purse: An analysis of Commercial Law issues associated with stored-value cards and electronic money report." The Business Lawyer. 52 (2), 653-727. Recovered from http://bit.ly/2Ikh53P [Links]

Tucker, P. (209). "The digital currency doppelganger: Regulatory challenge or harbinger of the new economy note". Cardozo Journal of International and Comparative Law. 17 (2), 589-626. Recovered from http://bit.ly/2Zs0vpP [Links]

Velde, F. (2013). "Bitcoin: First". Chicago Fed Letter. 317 . Recovered from http://bit.ly/2Xuc1QS [Links]

Come, N. (2018). Explaining the early responses to blockchain technology (master). University of Leiden, Leiden, The Netherlands. Recovered from http://bit.ly/2XzuCew [Links]

De Waal, B. (1995). Motivations for video game play: A study of social, cultural and physiological factors Simon Fraser University, Burnaby, Canada. Recovered from http://bit.ly/31bMHkX [Links]

Walch, A. (2016). "The path of the Blockchain lexicon (and the law) The Law of FinTech Symposium". Boston University Review of Banking and Financial Law. 36 , 1-13. Recovered from http://bit.ly/2QMX9KQ [Links]

Wang, H., Sun, C. (2011). "Game reward systems: Gaming experiences and social meanings". Think Design Play. 6 , 1-15. Recovered from http://bit.ly/2XuE7LF [Links]

Yamaguchi, H. (2004). "An analysis of virtual currencies in online games". SSRN Electronic

Journal. . Recovered from
http://doi.org/10.2139/ssrn.544422 [Links]

Yermack, D. (2015). "Is Bitcoin a real currency? An
economic appraisal". NBER Working Series. , 31-43.
Recovered from http://doi.org/10.3386/w19747 [
Links]

1 European Central Bank, "Electronic money",
European Central Bank, available at
http://bit.ly/2Yvlwz8 .

2 Golden Coin, for example, is a gold-backed digital
currency, but it requires both parties to hand over a
mandate to GCB Suisse AG, which claims to have
the backing gold that the parties trade. There are
many types of virtual currencies and for many
different purposes. The common factor of these
coins is in the appellation of "virtual" as opposed to
"real" or "backed".

3 Olga Kharif, «Forget airline miles. Crypto coins are coming to reward programs ", Bloomberg, May 30, 2018, available at https://bloom.bg/2YvguD4.

4 John Michael Makoto Dykes, "Digital cash and the development of the apolitical currency," MIT Computer Science & Artificial Intelligence Lab, 1995, available at http://bit.ly/2Yu7xts .

5 Denis Rice, "The past and future of Bitcoins in worldwide commerce," Business Law Today, November 11, 2013, available at http://bit.ly/2XpeKuO .

6I choose the evolution of online games instead of the evolution of electronic money, with respect to which crypto-currencies also reflect some improvements because I consider that what defines a crypto-currency is not the medium in which it is transmitted or its technological infrastructure, but what They have been designed with the express objective of becoming true "currencies" in an economic sense (currency), that is, a circulating means of payment with its own denomination that has a relative exchange value with respect to official money. For a brief history of electronic money in the United States that begins with the sending of "cables" by the telegraph, see Task Force on Stored-Value Cards (1996: 664-668). For discussions of Bitcoin as a currency, see Blundell-Wignall (2014), Halaburda and Sarvary (2016) and Yermack (2015).

7 Even in some communities, such as those of the Doom game, users generated improvements that they made, also free of charge, available to third parties (De Waal, 1995). This possibility of unlimited duplication was contrary to scarcity, an essential element of the means destined to transfer value and potentially to become circulating currencies.

8 Broadband transformed the gamer who could once be a star in his family or in his neighborhood by putting his initials on the winners' lists of consoles or flippers - in the style of players in Hollywood movies like The Last Starfighter or Cloak & Dagger — in recognized stars of larger virtual communities made up of strangers. For an

economic explanation of this phenomenon, see Jeremy Kelly, "Play time: The problem of abundance in MMORPG," Anthemion.org, available at http://bit.ly/2wBeGwe .

9 With the centralized power to save history and provide virtual "economic" goods (Shaviro, 2007), game developers created true virtual worlds with their own physical laws in which scarcity patterns were maintained, where users they lived, competed, enriched, associated, socialized and lost, to eventually be reborn as poor (Lastowka and Hunter, 2004).

10 According to Richard Bartle, father of the first multi-user Dungeons & Dragons derivative game, MUD1, in 1979, the first skill sale of a game was in 1987 in the game Shades. The sale was not of objects, but of abilities to obtain the category of magician. See Dan Hunter, "The early history of real money trades," Terra Nova, January 13, 2006, available at http://bit.ly/2YtnaS2 .

11 Mark Wallace, «The game is virtual. The profit is real ", The New York Times, May 29, 2005, available at https://nyti.ms/2YB4OP .

12 Mark Wallace, "The game."

13 Denis Rice, "The past."

14 Jeremy Kelly, "Play time."

15 For example, if Blizzard Entertainment, owner of World of Warcraft, decided to double the price of everything sold on the platform in its own currency, WoW Gold, or to halve the available goods, it would in practice have decreased halved the relative value of your currency.

16 Daniel Terdiman, "Virtual gaming's elusive exchange rates," CNET, August 5, 2005, available at https://cnet.co/2VFwY9Q. Platform developers do not normally use monopoly power over them to

defeat faith in their own virtual currencies. On the contrary, they use this power to extend the use of the platform, loyalty users and maximizing long-term profitability (Halaburda and Sarvary, 2016). To do this, they follow a strategy of setting their prices according to demand (Gans and Halaburda, 2015). This redirects the problem of the exchange rate of virtual currencies to the factors that affect the direct demand for virtual goods of the platforms, and in this equation the number of users and the pleasure that they produce playing the game or participate in the platform. Thus, the exchange rate of a virtual currency is determined by the popularity of the platform to which it is associated and by the willingness to play of its most experienced users or the willingness to pay of its most adept users (Shin, 2008). These users reap the rewards of the game or purchase them. With this, they signal through the time spent playing and through their payments in current money the sacrifice of goods required in the real world to obtain the scarce virtual goods that the platform produces and sells (Heeks, 2009; Yamaguchi, 2004).

17 In any case, a virtual currency whose advantage is to enable the purchase of goods in a game that

falls into disuse is a currency without even virtual support and whose value remains in the hands of the developer without any of the restrictions described. This problem could be solved, in part, by increasing the usability of virtual currencies on new platforms. If a developer or a group of them credibly and consistently allows users to migrate their digital wealth from one platform to the other, it would mitigate the exchange rate problem that plagues virtual currencies and make it easier for them to be used as a medium of exchange and store of value. This would amount to the creation of virtual private money with a preferred potential use: the superior experience in games and virtual worlds.

18 Initially, before broadband, there were attempts to deal with the problem of the middleman via encryption that blinds the transactions to the middleman in the case of electronic money. This encryption protected the identity of the parties and, therefore, at least partially, the potential malicious control over particular transactions (Chaum, 1992). But the idea, applied in experiments such as DigiCash, did not work commercially, since they were not attractive

enough to differentiate themselves from the credit cards that consumers knew, and that took advantage of the network effects to quickly take on e-commerce (Grinberg, 2012 : 169).

19 Kelly Grant, "Saving reward points and miles isn't a sound money strategy," CNBC, August 3, 2016, available at https://cnb.cx/2VCyhGC ; Daniel Terdiman, "Virtual".

20 There is abundant literature - to date more than 433 articles indexed in the Web of Science - on crypto-currencies and their advantages and disadvantages in various areas of knowledge. Four years ago there were only 15 articles indexed in that database (Spenkelink, 2014). Google Scholar and Scopus double this figure. The exhaustive review of all the existing articles is impractical and, due to the technical specialty in some areas, ineffective.

21 The main transaction unit of the Bitcoin currency is bitcoin (1 BTC), the smallest unit is a satoshi (equivalent to 0.000000001 BTC). From now

on I will use Bitcoin for the complete payment system and bitcoin for the unit of account or denomination of payments made with Bitcoin.

22 Jeff John Roberts, "How bitcoin is stolen: 5 commons threats," Fortune, December 8, 2017, available at http://bit.ly/2M4qZMl . A good graphical animated English representation of this process can be found on the "Blockhain demo" page of Anders Brownworth's blog, available at https://anders.com/blockchain/ .

23 Rich Apodaca, "Bitcoin: Think of it as electronic cash," Bitzuma, September 28, 2017, available at http://bit.ly/2Vz8wqA .

24 George Kimionis, reply to query "Can a wallet deny payments to it?" on Bitcoin Stack Exchange, January 8, 2015, available at https://bitcoin.stackexchange.com/a/35368 .

25 "Change", Bitcoin Wiki, July 25, 2017, available at https://en.bitcoin.it/wiki/Change .

26 The analogy between crypto-currencies and metallic currencies is admittedly thick, but the operation of transactions in Bitcoin is as if each coin were a bar or gold ingot that melts in each transaction, it melts again with a stamp that owners are passing each other, and it has the history of the addresses where that gold has been used since it was mined from the ground. In this operation, the owner can only claim dominion over the coins because he has in his possession the stamp that allows tracing the gold of the coin that he will melt to its origin. Rich Apodaca, "Bitcoin."

27 "Change", Bitcoin Wiki.

28 Vitalik Buterin, "Ethereum white paper: Next generation smart contract and decentralized platform." Brave New Coin, August 20, 2014, available at http://bit.ly/2liyxFY ; "Not-so-clever contracts," Schumpeter, The Economist, July 28, 2016, available at https://econ.st/2VCP2RJ .

29 Tom Espiner, "Is blockhain living up to the hype?", BBC News, October 23, 2018, available at https://bbc.in/2VDIwds.

30 The balance between ability and luck to close blocks reduces, in part, the possibility that these will always be closed by the same person and prevents the miner with the greatest computational processing power from actually becoming a controller of the transaction record (Bonneau and others, 2015).

31 An animated graphical presentation in English of this process can be seen on Anders Brownworth's blog "Blockhain demo".

32 Typically, since bitcoin transactions can be pending for a few minutes before being incorporated into a block, many electronic wallets require that a transaction be at least five or six blocks old before they are considered fully validated (Bonneau et al., 2015). The site http://data.bitcoinity.org provides real-time data on the delay in which the blocks are created and

the speed has been stable between nine and ten minutes, as designed. Therefore, for most users, 50 minutes is the time between transaction and transaction with the same currencies, without prejudice to the fact that all of them are irreversible between the parties from the moment they are generated.

33 Note that when there is no consensus among miners, they can work in parallel chains - with transactions that diverge - setting up what is called a fork in the chain. But since it is difficult for a chain containing invalid transactions to convince more than 50% of the network for long, especially in consolidated crypto-currencies such as Bitcoin, and since it continues to maintain a false and discrepant chain solving the mathematical problems required to growing it is, by design, uneconomical, discrepant chains eventually die and miners converge to the longest chain (Doguet, 2012: 1.127; Nakamoto, 2009: 3).

34 Patrik Korda, "Bitcoin bubble 2.0," Patrik Korda's Blog, March 5, 2013, available at http://bit.ly/2LZrEym ; Patrick Murphy, "On Bitcoin

and Ludwig von Mises' regression theorem," Free Advice, March 10, 2014, available at http://bit.ly/2M07eoY; Michael Suede, "The economics of Bitcoin - Challenging Mises' regression theorem," Libertarian News, July 7, 2011, available at http://bit.ly/2M3I88Q ; Peter Šurda, "Re: Bitcoin bubble 2.0 by Patrik Korda", Economics of Bitcoin, March 6, 2013, available at http://bit.ly/2LYZzqP .

35 Peter Šurda, "Re: Bitcoin".

36The miners' proof of work fits better with Adam Smith's conception of how wealth is generated and with the concept of scarcity, but in the virtual world. Smith noted that labor "was the primitive price, the original acquiring currency paid in the world for all interchangeable things. Not with gold, not with silver, but with work, all kinds of wealth were originally bought in the world (Smith, 1794: 50; see also Peach, 2009: 393). Crypto-currencies and their predecessors were born with virtual worlds and - as if their designers wanted to please Smith - with the scarcity programmed into them.

The work required to obtain the riches (real money trading,

37 The amount of crypto-currencies circulating, that is, the total value that you could buy with all the relevant crypto-currencies in their dollar value does not exceed 135.1 billion dollars as of March 2019, which is insignificant when compared to the 7 trillion dollars in gold reserves. Toju Ometoruwa, "Understanding crypto-currency market capitalization," MTC Manager, March 9, 2019, available at http://bit.ly/2M11nQj . Also the amount is negligible or with the physical 5 trillion US dollars circulating in the world. Mitchell Hartman, "Here's how much money there is in the world - and why you've never heard the exact number," Business Insider, November 17, 2017, available at http://bit.ly/2M2nwxO

38 The same states have faced competition from private currencies throughout history when they have faced financial weakness or lack of credibility. If, in most cases, state money has prevailed, it is because of monopoly coercion and because the states have made efforts to legally commit to

ensuring that their money retains its value beyond legally declaring its liberating power. For example, they have given their money the possibility of extinguishing public debts, which, as Wray points out, "is what is needed to pay taxes" (Barber, 2015). And they have guaranteed that they will compare and extinguish their currency "if its real value starts to fall much more than 2% a year" (Brad DeLong, "Watching Bitcoin, Dogecoin, etc ...", Washington Center for Equitable Growth, December 28, 2013 , available inhttp://bit.ly/2LZmGS9). Perhaps giants like Amazon or Facebook could try to impose their private currencies based on their prestige or the size of their captive networks and users without having the coercive power of the State and without having made a commitment to maintain the value of their currencies (Halaburda and Sarvary, 2016). Most private crypto-currency issuers who want to retain control of crypto-currencies will have to find ways to back them up if they want their creation to be accepted and partially relinquish control. They will try, for example, to establish a profit that can only be accessed with their currency or to try to tie it to a commodity. In the latter case, they must demonstrate that they have the commodity in sufficient quantities, something that so far all the creators of virtual currencies that have followed this strategy have failed to demonstrate (Roubini,

39 Bitcoin's success is sometimes described as the result of applying 'cryptoeconomics' techniques, which is applying knowledge of cryptography and economics to design robust protocols and applications that have incentives for human adopters who need to decide to participate in them. Specifically, cryptoeconomics would consist of the design of mechanisms that contain incentives for users to participate, and could be considered a subfield of microeconomics and game theory. Alex Evans, "A crash course in mechanism design for cryptoeconomic applications," Block Channel, October 16, 2017, available at http://bit.ly/2LZBcJI .

40 Whatever people say about early adopter idealism, the success of Bitcoin adoption is due to the financial incentives generated by the visionary community that sustained it. Joshua Davis, "The crypto-currency," The New Yorker, October 3, 2011, available at http://bit.ly/2M4ZXEn .

41 Michael Grothaus, "How to create your own crypto-currency," Fast Company, January 29, 2014, available at http://bit.ly/2MdoFCq . This is another characteristic of the evolution of the currency that Carl Menger anticipated more than a century ago: «Nothing has been more favorable to the genesis of a new medium of exchange than the acceptance by the most conscious and capable economic subjects who seek their own profit and for a good period of time, of an eminently liquid good »(Álvarez and Bignon, 2013: 98; own translation).

42 Vitalik Buterin, "Ethereum."

43 "Bitcoin scams and crypto-currency hacks list", Bitcoin Exchange Guide, available at http://bit.ly/2M12q2J.

44 Nathaniel Popper, "Bitcoin's Power Consumption Is Not Trivial", The New York Times, January 24, 2018, available at https://nyti.ms/2M2XOch .

Four. FiveSince Bitcoin was born in 2009, it has attracted the attention of numerous academics in the area of Anglo-Saxon law, both in areas of doctrine and jurisprudence, as well as in peripheral areas. In the Anglo-Saxon database Heinonline Law Journal Library, which contains 2,600 newspapers and academic journals related to law, there are already more than 551 that contain the word crypto-currencies or derivatives. (Data obtained using search results for "crytpocurr *" in HeinOnline Law Journal Library). Databases such as Scielo / Scopus (Spanish), Westlaw (Mexico), Westlaw (Chile), ScienceDirect (Spanish) combined yield a dozen articles in Spanish. Dialnet and Google Scholar in Spanish have hundreds of sources, but many of them correspond to non-indexed articles or brief analyzes in legal journals.

46 Judgment of the case "Preliminary procedure. Common system of value added tax (VAT). Directive 2006/112 / CE. Articles 2, section 1, letter c), and 135, section 1, letters d) to f). Services for consideration. Exchange operations of the virtual currency "bitcoin" for traditional currencies. Exemption ", Court of Justice of the European

Union, C - 264/14, October 22, 2015, available at http://bit.ly/2I6msF0 .

47 Kevin Helms, "How 5 Asian countries regulate crypto-currency," News, Bitcoin.com, April 8, 2019, available at http://bit.ly/2I6OWQO .

48 John Jeff Roberts, "How bitcoin."

49 Sergio Carrasco, «Can bitcoins or other virtual currencies be seized?», Derecho en Red, September 4, 2013, available at http://bit.ly/2M3bTqo .

50 Kevin Peachy, "Divorcing couples may clash over Bitcoin," BBC News, February 15, 2018, available at https://bbc.in/2M5fzYH .

51 For example, if a crypto-currency is backed by some commodity, the underwriting contracts that are returned to the bearer should be sufficient to

claim that they are convertible to the backing commodity. In these cases, it might only be convenient to monitor the reserve requirement or the reserves of the commodity offered to preserve the stability of the media. Similar reasoning can be applied to cases where anonymity is waived, or where authorized nodes or persons operate, and cases where the coin has a controller. Centralization is an advantage to regulate because it puts a face and address on the controller, to which rules similar to those applicable to private money can be imposed.

52 Rutland, E. (2017). Blockchain Byte. FINRA. R3 Research, 2.

53. Yang, X., Chen, Y., & Chen, X. (2019, July). Effective scheme against 51% attack on proof-of-work blockchain with history weighted information. In 2019 IEEE International Conference on Blockchain (Blockchain) (pp. 261-265). IEEE.

54. Upadhyay, S. N. (2014). Legal Consequences of a Minor's Agreement in India. Business Law Review, 35(4).

www.ingramcontent.com/pod-product-compliance
Lightning Source LLC
Chambersburg PA
CBHW040125150726
48005CB00015B/2371